Marilyn
Monroe

Gone, but not
Forgotten

Contents

MARILYN MONROE

First published in the UK in 2012 by Instinctive Product Development

© Instinctive Product Development 2012

www.instinctivepd.com

Printed in China

ISBN: 978-1-908816-42-9

Designed by: BrainWave

Creative Director: Kevin Gardner

Written by: Jessica Bailey

Images courtesy of PA Photos, Shutterstock and Wiki Commons

Chapter 1:
On Screen

Some of Marilyn Monroe's films are described below in chronological order.

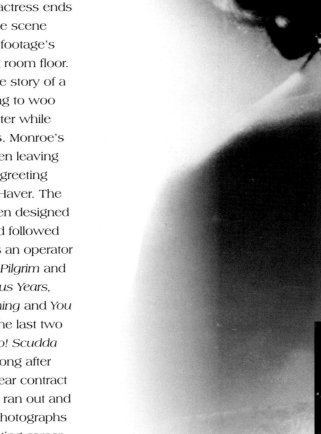

The 1948 movie *Scudda Hoo! Scudda Hay!* is generally considered to be Monroe's film debut – although the actress ends up with a brief one line scene following most of the footage's demise on the cutting room floor. The plot surrounds the story of a farmhand who is trying to woo his employer's daughter while also taming his mules. Monroe's character is briefly seen leaving a church service and greeting Rad, played by June Haver. The part had originally been designed over three scenes and followed her uncredited role as an operator in *The Shocking Miss Pilgrim* and brief roles in *Dangerous Years*, *Green Grass Of Wyoming* and *You Were Meant For Me*. The last two films, like *Scudda Hoo! Scudda Hay!*, were released long after Monroe's initial one-year contract with 20th Century Fox ran out and she posed nude for photographs while pursuing her acting career.

Scudda Hoo! Scudda Hay! (1948)

FACTS:

Written by:	F Hugh Herbert (based on the novel by George Agnew Chamberlain)
Directed by:	F Hugh Herbert
Released:	3 April 1948
Also starring:	June Haver, Walter Brennan, Lon McCallister

■ **RIGHT:** Lon McCallister and Walter Brennan who also starred in the movie with a young Elizabeth Taylor.

All About Eve (1950)

FACTS:

Written by:	Joseph L Mankiewicz
Directed by:	Joseph L Mankiewicz
Released:	13 October 1950
Also starring:	Bette Davis, Anne Baxter, Celeste Holm, George Sanders, Thelma Ritter

This 1950 drama from Joseph L Mankiewicz was based on the short story *The Wisdom Of Eve* (1946) by Mary Orr. Davis plays Margo Channing, a high-profile aging Broadway star, supported by a sound cast, while the film also provided Monroe with one of her most important roles to date. The film was praised by critics and public alike and was eventually nominated for 14 Academy Awards – a record at the time – and went on to win six in total including Best Picture. The film received four female acting nominations for Davis, Baxter, Holm and Ritter, which is still unmatched in Oscar history. The film was selected for preservation in the National Film Registry (US) in 1990 and appeared on the American Film Institute's list of the 100 Best American Films in 1998.

■ **ABOVE: Bette Davis is shown in a scene from the film, *All About Eve*.**

As Young As You Feel (1951)

FACTS:

Written by:	Lamar Trotti (screenplay), Paddy Chayefsky (original story)
Directed by:	Harmon Jones
Released:	11 April 1952 (France)
Also starring:	Thelma Ritter, Constance Bennett, David Wayne

■ **RIGHT:** Anne Bancroft.
■ **BELOW:** Director, Roy Ward Baker.

As Young As You Feel was Monroe's assignment under new contract with 20th Century Fox. Her first contract was signed by both parties in August 1946. The plot centres around 65-year-old John Hodges' elaborate scheme to avoid forced retirement from his job at a large motor company. The comedy is full of complications surrounding the age of retirement, which seems to have been completely captured by Fox in this unpretentious film. As well as concentrating on the frustrations of old age, the movie also portrays big business in the US and the relationships between husbands and wives. Having gleaned that no-one at his firm knows what the company boss looks like, Hodges takes it on himself to masquerade as the man in charge. Monroe plays Hodges' secretary – the topic of boss and secretary is also portrayed in the film – and wins critical acclaim for her portrayal.

Don't Bother To Knock was the first film for actress Anne Bancroft, while for Monroe it was her 18th time on set. It was also a chance for the up and coming Monroe to prove to her critics that she could act. With working titles of *Mischief* and *Night Without Sleep*, the film was a thriller which saw Monroe cast as Nell Forbes, the niece of elevator operator Eddie who works in a hotel. It is here that she is found babysitting Bunny, the daughter of Peter and Ruth Jones. Meanwhile, airline pilot Jed Towers (Richard Widmark)

is on his way to the same hotel to discuss the breakup of his relationship with bar singer Lyn Lesley. Towers and Forbes meet and it becomes apparent that the shy, but disturbed, girl should not be in charge of a child. The plot thickens around the darkness of Monroe's character and provides dramatic suspense while the story unfolds around her. Towers, who lost his relationship with Lesley (as she believes he does not have an understanding heart), is reunited with the bar singer when he persuades Nell that she should not take her own life.

Don't Bother To Knock (1952)

FACTS:

Written by:	Daniel Taradash
Directed by:	Roy Ward Baker
Released:	18 July 1952
Also starring:	Richard Widmark, Anne Bancroft, Donna Corcoran, Jeanne Cagney

Monkey Business (1952)

FACTS:

Written by:	Billy Wilder, IAL Diamond, Ben Hecht (play), Charles Lederer (screenplay)
Directed by:	Howard Hawks
Released:	5 September 1952
Also starring:	Cary Grant, Ginger Rogers, Charles Coburn

Many compare *Monkey Business* to the 1938 film *Bringing Up Baby*, which also starred Cary Grant (with direction from Howard Hawks). On the film's release in 1952, critics also made much of the fact that Rogers took the leading role when scenes between Grant and Monroe proved more believable. Even Hawks was unconvinced when the film was finally produced and was cited as saying that the movie was not as funny as

■ **LEFT: Cary Grant and Marilyn in the Howard Hawks farce *Monkey Business*, in 1952.**

Niagara (1953)

FACTS:

Written by:	Charles Brackett, Richard L Breen, Walter Reisch
Directed by:	Henry Hathaway
Released:	21 January 1953
Also starring:	Joseph Cotten, Jean Peters, Max Showalter

■ **ABOVE: Marilyn Monroe on the beach in *Niagara*.**

it could have been. Sometimes referred to as *Howard Hawks' Money Business* to avoid confusion with the Marx Brothers 1931 film of the same name, the plot concentrates on Grant's character Dr Barnaby Fulton, a research chemist working on a 'fountain of youth pill'. Esther, the chimpanzee, manages to find the rejuvenating effect by accident when she pours some chemicals into a water cooler after becoming loose in the laboratory. The film's comic edge is provided by the antics of all those drinking water from the cooler before it all works out in the end.

Niagara was a success and Monroe received critical acclaim for her femme fatale character plotting to murder her husband (played by Cotten); however, she was suffering from severe stage fright during filming. Under Hathaway's instructions, Monroe was comforted by make-up artist Allan 'Whitey' Snyder who was charged with making sure the actress made it on to the set. Despite this, it was becoming apparent that Monroe had the ability to appear overtly sexual on set and it was during the making

of *Niagara* that she developed 'the look' which would transcend into her following films.

The film itself was a dramatic thriller with a number of film noir elements and became a huge success for 20th Century Fox as well as providing the actress with one of the highlights of her career. Monroe is the movie's main character and hugs the limelight for much of its 92 minutes. Although unsubstantiated, *Niagara* is believed to be the inspiration for Hitchcock's *Vertigo* in 1958.

■ **BELOW:** Marilyn and Jane Russell appear in *Gentlemen Prefer Blondes*.

■ **ABOVE:** Marilyn tries on a new costume for her latest film *Gentlemen Prefer Blondes*, as designer Billy Travilla studies the effect. Travilla created all the costumes she wears in the film.

Gentlemen Prefer Blondes was an adaptation of the 1949 stage musical of the same name and was released by 20th Century Fox. Its main stay is its comic gags and musical numbers, most notably *Diamonds Are A Girl's Best Friend*, sung by Monroe and probably the iconic moment for which the movie is best remembered. However, Russell's character Dorothy Shaw gained critical acclaim for her sharp wit as best friend to Lorelei Lee, played by Monroe. Writer Loos followed the film with a sequel to her novel *But Gentlemen Marry Brunettes* charting the further adventures of Dorothy and Lorelei and, in 1955, *Gentlemen Marry Brunettes*, again starring Russell, was released. Also starring Charles Coburn, Elliott Reid and Tommy Noonan, 1953's *Gentlemen Prefer Blondes* was granted both critical acclaim and financial success. Jane Russell is reported to have taken Monroe under her wing during filming and the two actresses became firm friends.

Gentlemen Prefer Blondes (1953)

FACTS:

Written by:	Anita Loos, Joseph Fields, Charles Lederer (screenplay)
Directed by:	Howard Hawks
Released:	18 July 1953
Also starring:	Jane Russell, Charles Coburn

■ **RIGHT & INSET:** Marilyn in character and promotion for *How To Marry A Millionaire.*

How To Marry A Millionaire was based on two plays with a music score provided by Alfred Newman. The movie became the first to be filmed in Cinemascope widescreen format and, as a comedy, proved to be a real hit for Monroe. The three leading ladies – played by Bacall, Grable and Monroe in the characters of Schatze Page, Loco Dempsey and Pola Debevoise respectively – rent a penthouse suite from affluent Freddie Denmark (played by David Wayne) in the hope of attracting, and eventually marrying, millionaires. The film charts the success and failures of each character's dates with prospective suitors while much of the movie's comedy is provided by Monroe, whose character is too vain to wear the glasses she needs. Being unable to see properly, Pola ends up on the wrong plane at the airport and finds herself seated next to Denmark who has no trouble in wooing her and persuading Pola to wear her glasses. The end of the film sees all three women matched to men they love with Bacall's character finding a millionaire. When he reveals his true value all three women faint!

How To Marry A Millionaire (1953)

FACTS:

Written by:	Nunnally Johnson (screenplay)
Directed by:	Jean Negulesco
Released:	5 November 1953
Also starring:	Lauren Bacall, Betty Grable

River Of No Return (1954)

FACTS:

Written by:	Frank Fenton
Directed by:	Otto Preminger
Released:	30 April 1954
Also starring:	Robert Mitchum

Director Otto Preminger was assigned the film as part of his contract with 20th Century Fox, but initially had no interest in the project until he read the screenplay and realised that leading roles from Mitchum and Monroe would add to the movie's potential. Much of the film was set in Banff National Park in Canada and the cast and crew departed for Calgary in June 1953. During production, problems soon became apparent between Preminger and Monroe's acting coach Natasha Lytess, who insisted on taking the star aside for instruction contrary to that of the film's director. Preminger had Lytess removed from set but Monroe called 20th Century Fox's Darryl F Zanuck directly and insisted that she would be unable to continue without the support of her coach. With Monroe's box office draw, Preminger's wishes were overruled and Lytess was reinstated. It would do the actress no favours and, having been humiliated on his own set, the director took out his anger and frustration on Monroe for the remainder of filming. In addition, Robert Mitchum's heavy drinking, the constant rain and an ankle injury of Monroe's further hampered production.

■ **LEFT:** Marilyn Monroe with her co-star Robert Mitchum.

■ **BELOW:** Donald O'Connor and Marilyn Monroe stepping lively to an Irving Berlin tune in *There's No Business Like Show Business*, in 1954.

There's No Business Like Show Business (1954)

FACTS:

Written by:	Lamar Trotti (story), Phoebe Ephron, Henry Ephron
Directed by:	Walter Lang
Released:	16 December 1954
Also starring:	Ethel Merman, Donald O'Connor

Released by 20th Century Fox, *There's No Business Like Show Business*, borrowed its name from the musical *Annie Get Your Gun* and the song of the same name. Based on the lives of vaudeville family the Donahues in 1919, the movie was a disappointment for the film company. Monroe had turned down the part of Victoria (Vicky) Hoffman and Sheree North was studio tested instead. However, Monroe eventually agreed to make the film when she was promised a leading role in *The Seven Year Itch*, directed by Billy Wilder. Merman first sang the leading song in the original Broadway production of *Annie Get Your Gun* some eight years before in 1946. The actress then sang it in the movie when her character Molly Donahue was reunited with her husband and son on stage with Vicky. The end of the film sees another huge hit *Alexander's Ragtime Band* sung by the Donahue family before the cast sing *There's No Business Like Show Business* for the movie's finale.

13

With the iconic footage of Monroe's dress billowing over a subway grate (although the actual scene used was shot over a sound stage), *The Seven Year Itch* was based on Axelrod's play of the same name. Ewell reprised his original Broadway part, while Monroe replaced Vanessa Brown as The Girl. The majority of the action takes place in the overactive imagination of Ewell's character Richard Sherman who has sent his wife and son to Maine in order to escape the scorching summer in the city. The Girl, a model, is renting the apartment upstairs while advertising toothpaste. Sherman is proofreading a book, claiming that many men have extra-marital affairs after seven years of marriage, by Dr Brubaker, a psychiatrist. He begins having imaginary conversations with The Girl in order to convince her that he is irresistible. He also has a fantasy that she is a femme fatale. Back in film reality, after having a drink, the two grow close but Sherman is convinced that his resolve to avoid temptation is proof that the seven year itch in marriage really does exist for men. Throughout the film, Sherman's fantasies render him completely paranoid. Finally, he comes to his senses and after telling The Girl she can stay at his apartment, he flees New York City for Maine.

■ **LEFT & BELOW:** Marilyn Monroe promoting *The Seven Year Itch*.

The Seven Year Itch (1955)

FACTS:

Written by:	George Axelrod and Billy Wilder
Directed by:	Billy Wilder
Released:	3 June 1955
Also starring:	Tom Ewell, Evelyn Keyes

Sadly, *The Prince And The Showgirl* did not achieve either critical acclaim or financial success and it would be 1970 before its director, Olivier, returned to directing motion pictures. The film is set in London around the time of the coronation of King George V in June 1911. Invited guests include the Prince Regent (played by Olivier) of Carpathia (a fictional Balkan country) who has less than moral intentions towards showgirl Elsie Marina, (played by Monroe) whom he meets at a performance of *The Coconut Girl*. His advances are rebuffed during a meal at the Carpathian embassy, however, following the coronation and a plot by the Prince Regent's son to overthrow him, the two main characters fall in love and relations are restored between father and son. Olivier was reportedly furious with the behaviour of Monroe throughout filming while, for the American actress, it was one of the few films she worked on outside of 20th Century Fox. The film was nominated for five BAFTA awards including Best British Actor, Best British Film, Best British Screenplay, Best Film from any source and Best Foreign Actress.

■ **RIGHT & BELOW:** Sir Laurence Olivier and Marilyn on the set of *The Prince And The Showgirl.*

The Prince And The Showgirl (1957)

FACTS:

Written by:	Terence Rattigan
Directed by:	Laurence Olivier
Released:	13 June 1957
Also starring:	Laurence Olivier, Richard Wattis, Sybil Thorndike

Some Like It Hot (1959)

FACTS:

Written by:	Billy Wilder, IAL Diamond
Directed by:	Billy Wilder
Released:	29 March 1959
Also starring:	Tony Curtis, Jack Lemmon

■ **ABOVE:** Marilyn Monroe on the set of *Some Like It Hot*.

■ **LEFT:** Leaving New York to start work on the film *Some Like It Hot*, her first film in two years.

Joe (Curtis) and Jerry (Lemmon), witness the Saint Valentine's Day massacre in Chicago, 1929. Seen by the gangsters themselves, the two musicians flee the city and end up in disguise in an all-girl band heading for Florida.

But complications ensue when both men fall for the band's vocalist, Sugar Kane, played by Monroe. Joe (now calling himself Josephine) takes on a second disguise as Junior, millionaire and heir to Shell Oil. Meanwhile,

Jerry, now masquerading as 'Daphne', attracts the attention of millionaire Osgood Fielding III, who proposes. In his excitement 'Daphne' accepts believing he will gain a large financial settlement following the wedding. The gangsters then arrive at the same hotel where the band are staying and comedy chases ensue while, at the same time, Joe reveals his true identity to Sugar who loves him anyway. 'Daphne' tries to explain to Osgood that they can't marry and is forced to announce: "I'm a man" to which the hapless groom replies: "Well, nobody's perfect".

■ **BELOW: Jack Lemmon, director Billy Wilder and Tony Curtis gather on the deck of the Hotel Coronado to celebrate the 25th anniversary of *Some Like It Hot*.**

The Misfits (1961)

FACTS:

Written by:	Arthur Miller
Directed by:	John Huston
Released:	1 February 1961
Also starring:	Montgomery Clift, Eli Wallach, Thelma Ritter, Clark Gable

The last film Marilyn Monroe starred in.

■ **ABOVE: Director John Huston, Marilyn Monroe and script writer Arthur Miller.**

■ **BELOW RIGHT: Winning all the money in the Hi-Fli competition.**

The Misfits received mixed reviews on its release in early 1961 and didn't achieve its expected commercial success. Set in Reno, the story concentrates on the love affair of Roslyn Taber, played by Monroe, and Clark Gable's character Gay Langland. A renowned rustler, Langland uses the proceeds of his ill-gotten gains to fund his gambling lifestyle and woo Taber, a depressed divorcee. Production of the film proved difficult in the heat of the Nevada desert, while director Huston made matters worse with his drinking, gambling and falling asleep on set. Filming was further hampered by the breakdown in Monroe's marriage to Arthur Miller. Clark Gable suffered a heart attack two days after filming ended and died 10 days later. Photographs of the film shoot, taken by Inge Morath (who went on to marry Miller), received worldwide critical acclaim. For his part, Miller's last play, *Finishing The Picture* (2004), was based on the production of the film. Despite its disappointing release, the film went on to receive cult status and is widely regarded by modern movie critics as a classic.

Chapter 2:
Marilyn Monroe

Born Norma Jeane Mortensen (although it was incorrectly spelled as Mortenson on her birth certificate) on 1 June 1926 to Gladys Pearl, the baby – who would become known to the world as Marilyn Monroe – took her initial surname from her mother's second husband, although he was undoubtedly not her father. Her mother's marriage to Martin E Mortensen had broken up in May 1925. Gladys' first marriage to John Newton Baker, which also ended in divorce, had resulted in two older children.

For the child, Monroe's father would remain a mystery, at least until she was in her mid-teens. But, that was far from the most pressing worry that would face the newborn baby. Just 12 days after she was born, Monroe was placed with her mother's neighbours Wayne and Ida Bolender who had fostered children for a number of years. Gladys had already lost her two older children, Robert and Berniece Baker, who had been abducted by their father. She wasn't about to abandon Norma Jeane altogether but, having had a hard life herself, Gladys seemed ill-equipped to deal with the small baby.

Gladys was born in 1902 to Otis and Della Monroe and, at the

■ **RIGHT: A young Marilyn pictured in 1928.**

age of seven, she had watched her father die at the California State Hospital for the mentally ill. It was later proved that Otis Monroe had in fact died of syphilis of the brain, but his family had believed – and continued to believe – that he had died insane. The mistaken poor mental health of Otis Monroe would blight the family and set the scene for Norma Jeane's own problems throughout her life.

While still married to Mortensen and working at Consolidated Film Industries, Gladys began an affair with recently divorced Charles Stanley Gifford. Gladys was left alone and bereft when Gifford announced that he was enjoying his newfound freedom too much to settle down again. But, Gladys was pregnant. Once Norma Jeane (named after a child in Kentucky that Gladys had looked after while chasing her abducted children) was born, mother and child moved closer to Della Monroe on East Rhode Island Avenue, Los Angeles and, in keeping with

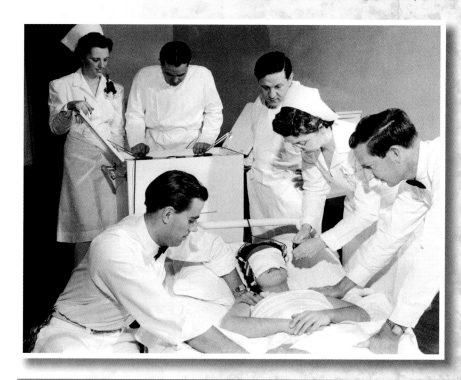

■ **ABOVE:** The California State Hospital, where a patient receives treatment.
■ **BELOW:** An RKO Regent movie theatre.

the fact that Gladys wished to be known by her first married name (Baker), the child's surname was changed.

It was Gladys' plan that the Bolenders could care for her child while she worked – by now she had taken a job at

Radio-Keith-Orpheum (RKO) – but long commutes, hard work and bringing up a baby as a single parent were proving too much for the former film cutter and she promptly moved back to Hollywood. Norma Jeane was left with the Bolenders where she

would stay for the next six years. A year after Norma Jeane's birth, Della died from manic depression in a mental hospital which further compounded the sense of insanity within the Baker/Monroe family. The Bolender family was willing and keen to adopt the small girl, but Gladys still visited her daughter on occasion and was not open to the idea. Norma Jeane, meanwhile, grew up in a confused environment where she wasn't sure whom her parents were. However, she was happy and content at 'home' and the Bolenders – despite reports to the contrary in the early days – were not responsible for the lack of emotional support that Monroe felt she suffered as a child. In fact, her own biological family were largely to blame with their inconsistent behaviour, lack of guidance, readiness to abandon Norma Jeane and constant talk about an insane heritage.

By the tender age of nine, Norma Jeane left the comfort of the Bolenders to move with her mother into the home of George and Maud Atkinson and their daughter Nellie. The carefree family came as somewhat of a shock to Norma Jeane who was used to a fairly strict environment where dancing, drinking and smoking were all considered sinful. It was while here that Monroe became interested in cinema and the movies and the legendary Jean Harlow. Her mother eventually bought a house and persuaded the Atkinsons to move in with her and her daughter. Monroe was bought a baby grand piano – she had learnt to play while living with the Bolenders – which would remain with her until the end of her life. But times were far from happy during this period. Gladys'

grandfather reportedly hung himself and her son died at the age of 15 from tuberculosis of the kidneys. Both events did little to settle Gladys' fragile state of mind and Monroe was left to deal with the aftermath of her mother's distress. It was a downward spiral from which both mother and daughter would not recover – at least not together.

Gladys was eventually hospitalised due to her mental

state and Monroe was badly affected by the demise in her mother's health. In September 1935, Monroe was taken to the Los Angeles Orphans Home. Over the coming years, Monroe was in and out of new foster homes as well as spending time living with her mother's friend, Grace Goddard, and a short spell with her paternal aunt, Ana Lower.

Childhood had been a struggle

- **ABOVE: Jean Harlow.**
- **LEFT: Clark Gable and Jean Harlow.**

she was. Having spent many years feeling unloved and abandoned, the attention that she was now gaining was intoxicating to the adolescent girl. Norma Jeane's guardians were powerless to stop the adoration that followed her and unsure of how to control her eagerness to please and encourage those that tried – both successfully and unsuccessfully – to become a part of her life.

Then, at the hands of Grace Goddard with approval from Ana Lower, a plan was hatched to provide Norma Jeane with safety and security. James (Jim) Dougherty (21), may have saved Norma Jeane (just 16 years old) from returning to the orphanage when the two youngsters married in 1942, but life was still out there for the future Marilyn Monroe and it was through her own courage and determination that she would find it.

of inconsistent love, both conditional and unconditional, for Monroe with no real permanent foundations. She had nothing to base her feelings on and people she thought were her parents (the Bolenders) turned out not to be. There were also times when there were no parental figures, including when she was sent to live in the orphanage, and some might argue that it is for these reasons – and nothing to do with the mental states of other family members – that Monroe suffered so greatly.

By the age of 12, Monroe was wearing tight clothing which just made it more noticeable that her rapidly developing figure was attracting the attention she so desperately craved. Whether it was from schoolboys, workmen or anyone walking past her on the street, Norma Jeane was marvelling at just how noticeable

Chapter 3:
Marilyn, Men and Marriage

First time lucky

Despite snatches of happiness on and off there had been much confusion, upset and moving around in Monroe's formative years. But, on 19 June 1942, at the tender age of 16 and still called Norma Jeane, she was offered the chance of stability through marriage to 21-year-old James Dougherty. The 'arranged' marriage was the brainchild of Grace Goddard and her neighbour Ethel Dougherty, the groom's mother. Marriage hadn't been in the minds of either of the intended but, with Grace's changing personal circumstances, Monroe was to be rid of foster homes and the orphanage with the offer of a groom who instantly set about convincing all concerned that the couple were very much in love.

The extremely young couple rented a small but neat house where they found happiness of a sort, although it is reputed that Dougherty did actually realise he had fallen in love with his wife. It was, perhaps, an unbalanced relationship when Monroe – having never had a solid father-figure in her life – became used to calling Dougherty 'daddy', and ensuring that his needs and wishes were met before her own. However, in *The Secret Happiness Of Marilyn Monroe*, Dougherty insists that the couple were in love but that his wife was lured away from him by dreams of stardom.

A year after the marriage, Monroe discovered that her father was Charles Stanley Gifford. Gladys had finally given her consent for Grace to break the news to her daughter. If the sudden revelation had a huge impact on Monroe it remained hers alone as she continued to be a diligent and proud housewife. Dougherty joined the US Navy and, in April 1944, Monroe landed a job while staying with her husband's parents, at Radioplane, an airplane factory, as a paint sprayer and parachute packer. Meanwhile, it is clear that Dougherty, having provided Monroe with some stability and a stab at normal life, had deferred his own decision to enlist in order to placate his young wife who was terrified by the prospect of losing her husband and the life they were building together. His eventual departure caused Monroe a direct blow to her self-worth and while on one level she seemed to have accepted and understood his need to join the Navy and serve his country in war, on another she blamed him for wrecking their relationship.

Dougherty had heaped love and praise on Norma Jeane and she was at a loss as to how to cope without it. Monroe panicked and, in a desperate attempt to persuade her husband not to leave her, announced that she would be contacting her father for the first time.

After Dougherty's departure and her arrival at Radioplane, Monroe regained some of her self-esteem through realising that she was needed and recognised in her role. It may also have shown the young woman that her marriage had been little more

■ **ABOVE: James Dougherty at his home in Auburn Maine, 2004. Dougherty died in 2005.**

than a way to provide her with some form of identity which she badly needed and craved. (Some nine years later in 1953, Dougherty would claim in an article for *Photoplay* that Monroe had threatened to jump off the Santa Monica Pier if he ever left her.) However, Norma Jeane seems to have coped pretty well once her husband embarked on his first tour of duty.

Monroe was a diligent and dedicated worker who came to the attention of David Conover, a photographer, in June 1945. He had arrived at the factory to take pictures of women workers supporting the war effort and quickly discovered that Monroe was a natural in front of the camera. In fact, so comfortable was the paint sprayer that she began suggesting ways in which she might pose for the camera around the factory locations. She appeared in *Yank* magazine with the strapline 'Mrs Norma Jeane Dougherty'.

Dougherty may well have been right in his suggestion that Monroe was lured by the promise of stardom. It was apparent to both Conover and Monroe that modelling and perhaps the movies could provide her with a career and it was at this point that the aspiring young woman's dedication to her absent husband seems to have waned. Dougherty began to receive far fewer letters from his wife and eventually learned that she had quit her job with Radioplane in order to pursue her own goals. Dougherty did make an effort upon his return to woo back his wife but their differences were marked. He had little interest or understanding in the life that Monroe wanted and the success she had garnered in his absence. The marriage was

■ **LEFT:** Mrs Norma Jean Dougherty pictured in *Yank* magazine.

over just six months after Monroe first stepped in front of the camera, although the divorce was only granted in September 1946.

Just months after the divorce, Dougherty remarried, while Monroe refused to see her first marriage as that important with a constant dismissal of any feelings she might have had for her husband. It became

quite apparent that the budding model felt her marriage had held her back.

Dougherty went on to claim in later years that it was he who was her true love and the one who created the star 'Marilyn Monroe', however he did admit that he had been asked by his mother to marry Norma Jeane to avoid her being placed in an orphanage yet again. One of the police officers who attended the scene when Monroe's body was found knew Dougherty and phoned his friend to break the news. He didn't attend Monroe's funeral.

Just 12 months after starting work as a professional photographer's model, Norma Jeane signed her first movie contract with 20th Century Fox in 1946. Her name changed to Marilyn Monroe and modelling, it seemed, had just been that first crucial step towards an acting career. During the next three years, while showing little promise as an actress, Monroe supported herself through modelling jobs, photographs and appearing on the front covers of magazines. She took courses in dancing, singing and acting but the fame (and fortune) she craved during her early years somewhat eluded her. Her early film

appearances were minor, but her performances were well received. She enrolled at the University of California, Los Angeles (UCLA) in 1951 where she studied literature and art appreciation – there were already a number of films under her belt (some uncredited) – and she began appearing in other films alongside more established actors including Mickey Rooney and Dick Powell. That same year, Monroe was a presenter at the 23rd Academy Awards while, in 1952, she appeared on the cover of *Look* magazine as part of activities celebrating women joining UCLA.

■ **BELOW: Man of all talents Mickey Rooney.**

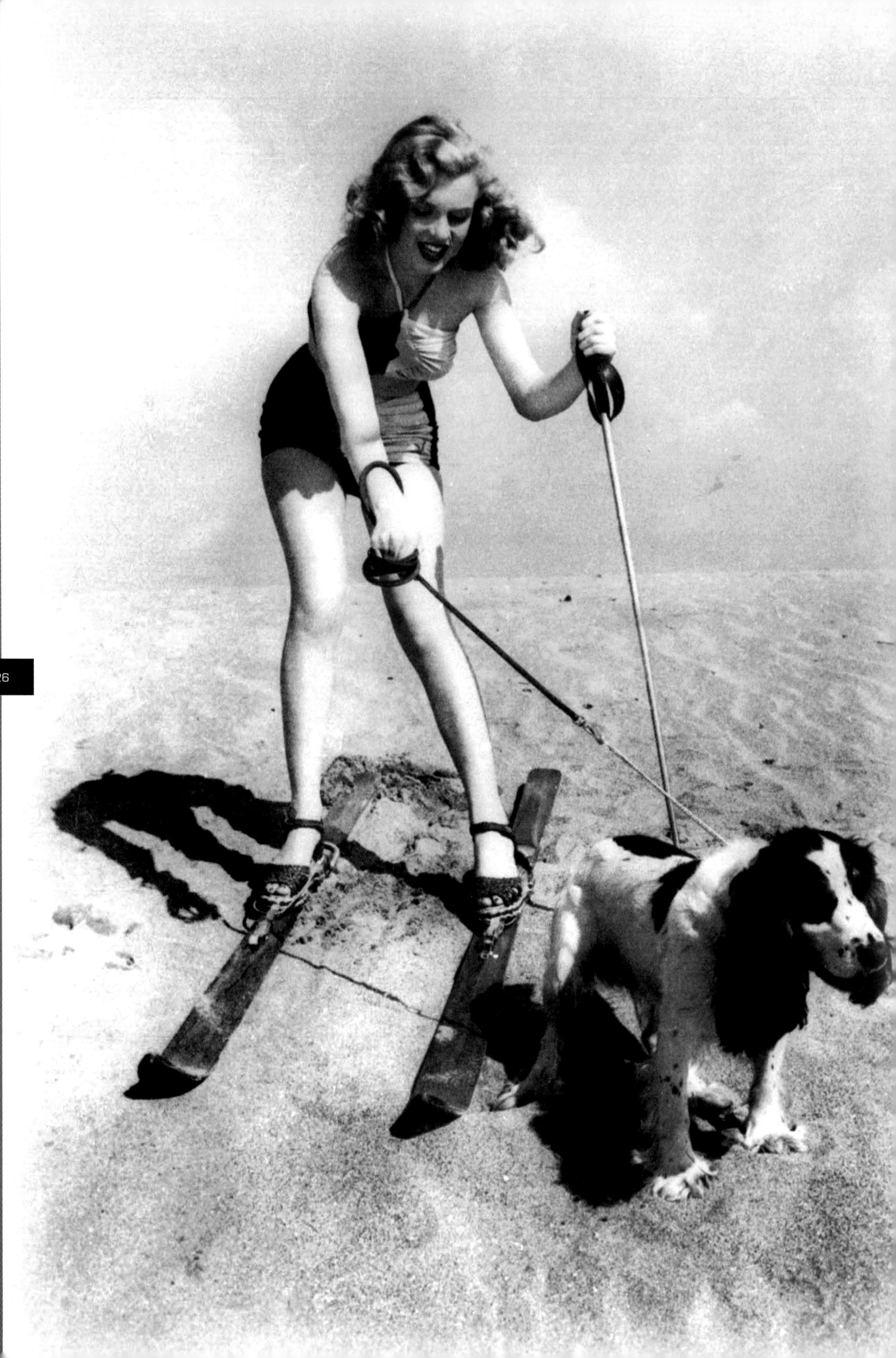

Joe DiMaggio

Towards the end of 1945, Monroe was signed to a modelling agency owned by Emmeline Snively, where she showed promise and dedication to her craft. Indeed, Norma Jeane was becoming a perfectionist and was desperate to know where the poses didn't quite work or where she had made mistakes. Her work ethic was second to none and Monroe was punctual, well prepared and hard working on set. Her sexual appeal was openly apparent, as was her ease in front of the camera and her sensuality, which exuded from

■ **LEFT: Starlet Marilyn at the beach with her dog Ruffles in 1947.**

her portfolio. However, Norma Jeane was far from Marilyn Monroe. At this point, her front teeth were still slightly protruding, her jaw line uneven and her hair frizzy brown. Yet, the style and the elegance, which were not far away, were evident in those early shots.

By early 1946, Norma Jeane had come to the attention of André de Dienes who photographed her in 'landscape' shots capturing her youthfulness. He was impressed with the young model and admired her self-assurance in front of the camera. However, he was baffled by her frailty and lack of awareness in her environment away from the camera's lens. It is well known that de Dienes had

a notion that Monroe would fall in love with him, but he was to be disappointed when she preferred to date a series of young men with whom she shared a passion for Hollywood.

One such ambitious man was Robert Slatzer who became friendly with Monroe when they met at 20th Century Fox in mid-1946. Slatzer cited that they had an on-off relationship and shared a love of poetry. It seems that in Slatzer, Monroe had found someone in whom to confide rather than to fall in love with but Bill Burnside, another of her new friends, confirmed her love of poetry, particularly the works of Keats and Shelley. It was during the mid-1940s that Monroe started to build up a small

library, with help from a circle of friends. Her love of books would further her educationally, professionally and personally. It is thought that any relationship she might have been tempted to have with de Dienes at this point would have damaged the future. The photographer was commanding and manipulative, whereas the likes of Slatzer

tolerated her moods and seemed to be happy supporting Monroe in whichever way suited her needs at the time. More than likely, despite his prowess and success, Monroe regarded de Dienes and his photographs of her as just another step towards her ultimate goal.

Joe DiMaggio, was introduced to a picture of Monroe posing

with Joe Dobson and Gus Zernial of the Chicago White Sox in 1951. A year later, while filming *Monkey Business*, Monroe agreed through mutual friend David March to meet the sporting hero. She had been slightly concerned that DiMaggio would prove to be a stereotypical sportsman but was pleasantly surprised that he wasn't at all egotistical. However, she refused a second date. Monroe was to write in *My Story* that she had never particularly wanted to meet DiMaggio in the first place, fearing his reputation and personality would all be too much for her; they were fears that would be unfounded.

Eventually, after DiMaggio's

■ **LEFT: Maj. Gen. William F Dean, who was held in captivity for more than three years by the North Korean Communists, jokes with Marilyn Monroe, Joe DiMaggio (left) and comedian Bob Hope (right) at a party at Hope's home in Hollywood.**

retirement from baseball and having agreed to a second date after all, Monroe found happiness in her blooming relationship with the sporting legend. But, it was during this time that 20th Century Fox would discover that their starlet had a little secret. Nude pictures of Monroe began to surface in Hollywood and could have had an adverse affect on her career. However, her declaration that she had been penniless and desperate at the time soon persuaded her bosses and a wider audience that a few naked shots were not worth ruining a potentially successful career for.

By the end of 1952, Monroe and DiMaggio were very much in love, but it was evident in his handling of those around his new lover that he was controlling and manipulative. It is well known that DiMaggio was much disliked by Natasha Lytess, Monroe's drama coach, having refused her request to let her speak to her pupil. He suggested that Lytess speak to Monroe's agent instead. Over the coming two years, Monroe and DiMaggio became totally wrapped up in each other and it was clear for all to see that their lives outside of each other meant nothing to either one. Monroe was completely uninterested in DiMaggio's past and his sporting achievements. Equally, DiMaggio disliked the dazzling energy of Hollywood and all that it stood for. When Monroe accepted DiMaggio's proposal of marriage on New Year's Eve 1953 at his family home in San Francisco, it was just 14 days before they tied the knot at City Hall in January 1954. The couple's honeymoon in Japan – where DiMaggio was assigned to coach baseball – would provide the beginning of the end for the newlyweds.

29

■ **ABOVE: Marilyn demonstrates perfect form at the plate as she waits for her pitch.**

■ **LEFT: Marilyn sets to work on her hand prints for the walk of fame.**

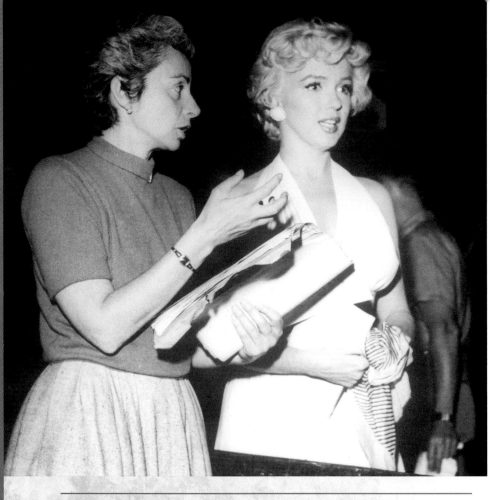

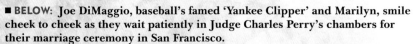

■ **ABOVE:** Marilyn Monroe with her acting coach Natasha Lytess on location in *The Seven Year Itch*.

■ **BELOW:** Joe DiMaggio, baseball's famed 'Yankee Clipper' and Marilyn, smile cheek to cheek as they wait patiently in Judge Charles Perry's chambers for their marriage ceremony in San Francisco.

During the visit, Monroe was requested to fly to Korea to perform 10 shows over four days for around 100,000 servicemen as part of United Service Organisation's (USO) activities for troops stationed in the country. Providing morale and recreational support, Monroe was a great success in Korea.

DiMaggio was less than impressed with his wife's support for the USO – he felt neglected –

and he was thrown by the lack of control it gave him over her. It is well cited that from this point on the marriage was in trouble. But, it seems that while filming *The Seven Year Itch* in New York (September 1954), DiMaggio was pushed over the edge by the media circus created by Monroe's skirt-blowing scene over the subway grate. There was a huge row between the pair which resulted in Monroe filing

■ **ABOVE:** Marilyn Monroe sings for a huge audience of GI's during a show at an American camp in Korea.

■ **ABOVE INSET:** Marilyn autographs a life-sized picture of herself for the men of the 2nd Division during her tour of the front-line divisions in Korea.

■ **LEFT:** Newlyweds Joe DiMaggio and Marilyn Monroe arrive at the International Airport, 29 January 1954, prior to their departure for Tokyo for an extension of their honeymoon. They were married in San Francisco on 14 January, and Marilyn was under suspension by her studio for failing to start a new picture.

■ **FAR LEFT:** Marilyn Monroe poses over the updraft of a New York subway grating while in character for the filming of *The Seven Year Itch*.

■ **LEFT:** Former baseball star Joe DiMaggio and Marilyn walk hand in hand as they arrive for the preview of Marilyn's new picture, *The Seven Year Itch*. Marilyn and hubby Joe, from whom she'd separated, looked like they were getting along fine.

■ **BELOW:** Marilyn appearing with the USO Camp Show, *Anything Goes*, poses for the shutterbugs after a performance.

for divorce on the grounds of mental cruelty just 274 days after the wedding.

During 1955, Monroe began studies at the Actors Studio where she suffered greatly from stage fright. The actress became firm friends with Eli Wallach and Kevin McCarthy, who both remembered her dedication and sincere approach to her art. She was also renowned for trying to remain unnoticed at the back of the acting classes. Run by Lee Strasberg, Monroe was eventually picked to give a performance of *Anna Christie* by Eugene O'Neill

in front of her peers alongside fellow student Maureen Stapleton. Rehearsals, prior to performance, were difficult and fraught and Monroe suffered from not managing her lines particularly well. However, come the time of the actual performance, Monroe made the whole thing seem effortless. It was during this time that Lee Strasberg was to comment that of the hundreds of students he had worked with, Marlon Brando was the best; Monroe came a close second.

Back in her personal life, marriage to DiMaggio had been difficult and fraught and there was even suspicion that the former baseball player had been violent on occasion; Monroe had been known to turn up on set with various bruises. But when she was admitted to the Payne Whitney Psychiatric Clinic early in 1961, it was DiMaggio who secured her release. She joined her former husband in Florida for a time when he was coaching at the New York Yankees' training camp. In 1962, it is believed that DiMaggio – who was worried by the company Monroe was keeping – was going to ask her to marry him for a second time.

After Monroe's death, DiMaggio arranged the star's funeral. Upon auction of his own effects in 2006, one photograph was signed, "I love you Joe. Marilyn".

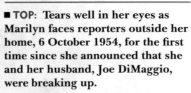

■ **TOP:** Tears well in her eyes as Marilyn faces reporters outside her home, 6 October 1954, for the first time since she announced that she and her husband, Joe DiMaggio, were breaking up.

■ **ABOVE:** Marilyn waits in the courtroom of the Superior Court building in Santa Monica, about to take the stand and testify in her divorce action against her husband, Joe DiMaggio.

■ **LEFT:** Marilyn leaves Columbia-Presbyterian medical centre in New York on 5 March 1961 after a long rest and checkup.

■ **RIGHT:** Marilyn and ex-husband, Joe DiMaggio, walk the shores of a beach near Sarasota, 1961.

Arthur Miller – Monroe's final marriage

Monroe first met Arthur Miller in Hollywood in 1951 when he arrived in LA with director Elia Kazan. Despite Monroe becoming Kazan's lover, Monroe and Miller became close and the playwright found himself quite distressed

■ **RIGHT:** Marilyn Monroe and her playwright husband Arthur Miller walking in the peace of the garden at Englefield Green, Surrey.

■ **BELOW:** Marilyn poses with Arthur Miller, in Roxbury, USA, shortly before their wedding.

by his feelings for her. After an extremely brief affair with the actress, an already married Miller quickly returned home to his wife and two children. However, in 1956, having left his first wife Mary Slattery, Miller married Monroe in New York City on 29 June. The ceremony itself was a low-key and quiet affair, held in the offices of lawyer Sam Slavitt. This first 'wedding' was kept a

■ **RIGHT:** The secret wedding of Marilyn Monroe to playwright Arthur Miller.

35

■ ABOVE: Marilyn greets English actor Sir Laurence Olivier with a kiss on the cheek, watched by his wife Vivien Leigh (left) and Monroe's husband Arthur Miller (right).

■ LEFT: Tony Curtis, who was alleged to have made Marilyn pregnant.

secret from both the press and the public, but a more formal Jewish ceremony (Monroe had converted to Judaism before her marriage) took place on 1 July in front of 30 invited guests with a reception hosted by Miller's literary agent, Kay Brown.

Within two weeks, the newlyweds were greeted in London by Monroe's forthcoming co-star, Laurence Olivier and his wife Vivien Leigh, for the filming of The Prince And The Showgirl. The press in London went into a frenzy at the arrival of the Hollywood icon. Monroe's behaviour during her time in the UK did little to enhance her image with Olivier, but her

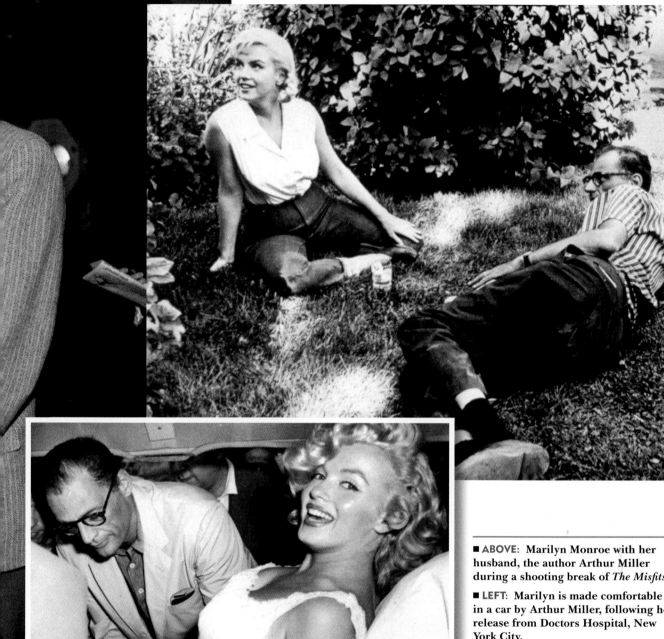

- **ABOVE:** Marilyn Monroe with her husband, the author Arthur Miller during a shooting break of *The Misfits*.
- **LEFT:** Marilyn is made comfortable in a car by Arthur Miller, following her release from Doctors Hospital, New York City.
- **BELOW:** Photographer Inge Morath, third wife of playwright Arthur Miller.

husband witnessed: "A whirling light... all paradox and enticing mystery..." After shooting was over, the couple returned to the US to discover that Monroe was pregnant. (She had been pregnant by Miller's friend Kazan, during their illicit affair, but the pregnancy had ended in miscarriage. Co-star, Tony Curtis, from *Some Like It Hot*, claims to have got Monroe pregnant in 1959 while she was still married to Miller. All Monroe's pregnancies ended in miscarriage, probably as a result

of the endometriosis suffered by the actress.)

Undeterred by a failing marriage and rumours of affairs and illegitimate pregnancies, Miller wrote *The Misfits* for his wife. However, by the time filming began in 1960, the romance that had begun almost a decade earlier was dwindling and the marriage was in tatters. The couple were granted a divorce in January 1961 and, less than a month later, Miller married photographer Inge Morath.

The Kennedys

Monroe is reported to have had affairs with President John F Kennedy and his brother Senator Robert Kennedy, both married men at the time. Much has been written and documented about these relationships; the mistress of the president, Judith Exner, even wrote about Monroe and Kennedy's affair in her autobiography, published in 1977.

One of the most prolific writers on the subject is Anthony Summers who wrote two books, both in the form of biographies about Monroe (*Goddess –*

■ **RIGHT:** John F Kennedy and his brother Robert Kennedy.

■ **BELOW:** Judith Campbell Exner is shown in 1960, the year she said she met John F Kennedy. Exner admitted to being a mistress of the late President, and that she acted as messenger to mob boss Sam Giancana, carrying what she believed were messages plotting the assassination of Cuban leader Fidel Castro.

■ **BELOW RIGHT:** Actor Peter Lawford and his bride, the former Patricia Kennedy, are all smiles as they sit in their limousine following their wedding in St Thomas More Roman Catholic Church on New York's Park Avenue, 24 April 1954.

MARILYN MONROE

published in 1985) and J Edgar Hoover, Director of the FBI (entitled *Official and Confidential: The Secret Life of J Edgar Hoover* some eight years later in 1993). Along with Summers, other writers also claim that Monroe was in love with President Kennedy and wanted to marry him in early 1960 but turned to his brother, Robert, when the dynamic leader of the US broke off their affair.

Patricia Kennedy Lawford, sister of John and Robert, was married to Peter Lawford. Patricia was the actor's first wife. The relationships between Monroe and the Kennedys are also discussed in *The Peter Lawford Story*, the biography of his life by his fourth wife, Patricia Seaton Lawford, who was close to the Kennedys at the time of Monroe's death.

Monroe made her last, high profile, public appearance at a birthday party held in honour of President Kennedy. It was 19 May 1962, the venue was Madison Square Garden, and a leading light who had less than three months to live sang her famous *Happy Birthday* to one of the world's most prominent leaders.

■ **ABOVE:** Marilyn Monroe's "Happy Birthday, Mr President" dress on display at Christie's in New York, 1999. The full-length, flesh-coloured dress, is hand sewn with more than 6,000 beads.

■ **RIGHT:** Marilyn speaks with John F Kennedy and Robert Kennedy (left) at a private party after her 1962 *Happy Birthday* song to US President John F Kennedy at Madison Square Garden in New York.

Chapter 4:
The Leading Men (and Ladies) of a Hollywood Icon

Despite a short-lived, if glittering, career (it spanned just 15 years), Monroe worked with some of the most prolific Hollywood actors of the 20th Century.

Cary Grant, named the second Greatest Male Of All Time by the American Film Institute, was one of Monroe's first leading men in *Monkey Business*, which also starred **Ginger Rogers**. The Bristol-born actor had made his name in the US with films such as *Bringing Up Baby* (1933), *Only Angels Have Wings* (1939) and later classics including *An Affair To Remember* in 1957 and *North By Northwest* that same year. Grant and Monroe were reported to have worked well together. Ginger Rogers – who made a total of 73 films – was particularly noted for the 10 musical movies that she made with Fred Astaire. The actress was an exceptional comic who, despite suffering from a lack of parts for older women, gave a solid performance in *Monkey Business*.

Richard Widmark had top billing alongside **Charles Laughton** and Monroe for *O'Henry's Full House*, made by 20th Century Fox in 1952. Widmark was fairly stereotyped during his early career as a

■ **RIGHT: Cary Grant.**

MARILYN MONROE

■ **LEFT: Richard Widmark.**
■ **BELOW: Charles Laughton.**

villainous or anti-hero character, particularly in films noir, but he managed to branch out in various westerns and mainstream dramas later on in his working life with memorable leading and support roles. Known for his presence on screen, stage, radio and TV, Widmark has a star on the Hollywood Walk of Fame and was inducted into the Western Performers Hall of Fame in 2002, some six years before his death, and the National Cowboy & Western Heritage Museum in Oklahoma City.

Playing husband to Monroe's femme fatale in *Niagara*, Joseph Cotten was also a star in his own right in films such as 1943's *Shadow Of A Doubt*, *Love Letters* (1945), *Portrait Of Jennie* three years later and *The Third Man* in 1949. The American actor was somewhat overshadowed by the sensual performance given by Monroe in this dark and foreboding movie. The release of *Niagara* took Monroe to her next venture and *Gentlemen Prefer Blondes* in 1953 where she starred with huge star, Jane Russell. It is well documented that, despite her rising success, Marilyn found it difficult to turn up on time to set and often appeared to have forgotten her lines. Russell was extremely patient with Monroe and the two actresses became firm friends despite their differences in treatment from 20th Century Fox; Monroe earned around $18,000 for the movie whereas Russell was reported to have made nearer $100,000.

Betty Grable and Lauren Bacall were Monroe's next co-stars in *How To Marry A Millionaire* also

■ **BELOW:** Jane Russell during the filming of some gymnasium scenes for *Gentlemen Prefer Blondes*.

starring David Wayne, Rory Calhoun, William Powell and Fred Clark in 1953, which won a BAFTA for Best Film (1955). As well as becoming one of Hollywood's best, Grable was also the ultimate pin-up during the Second World War when she posed in an iconic photograph in her bathing suit. The photo went on to appear in a project for *Life* magazine called '100 Photos That Changed The World'.
The actress' legs were particularly stunning and were insured by her studio with Lloyd's of London for a staggering $1 million. Meanwhile, 'husky' and 'sultry' Bacall made her film debut in film noir, where she gained much critical acclaim for her roles in *The Big Sleep* and *Dark Passage* in 1946 and 1947 respectively. But Bacall was also a good comic and won high praise for her role in *How To Marry A Millionaire*. The actress went on to be nominated for an Academy Award for *The Mirror Has Two Faces* in 1996 and was awarded a Golden Globe Award. In 2009, Bacall was awarded an Academy Honorary Award at the Governors' Awards.

In 1954, having been rebuffed by 20th Century Fox's Zanuck for a part in *The Egyptian*, Monroe was given a starring role in the western *River Of No Return*, opposite Robert Mitchum. Set in 1875, in the Northwest of the US, widower Matt Calder (played by Mitchum) returns

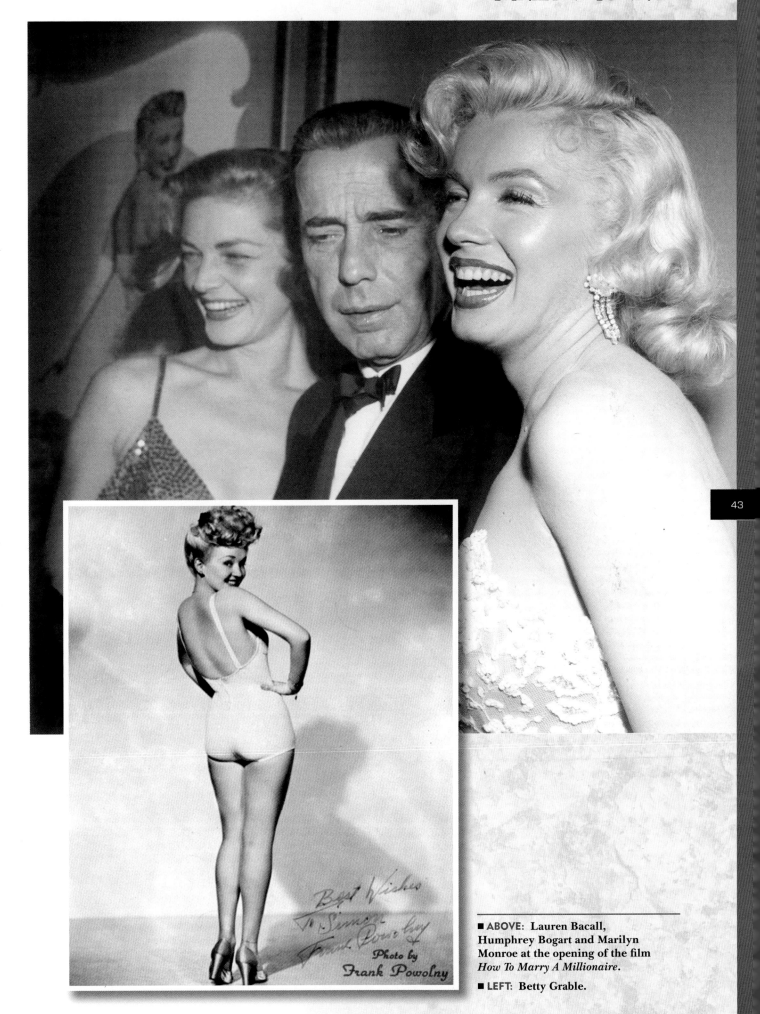

Best Wishes
To Simon
Frank Powolny

Photo by
Frank Powolny

■ **ABOVE:** Lauren Bacall,
Humphrey Bogart and Marilyn
Monroe at the opening of the film
How To Marry A Millionaire.

■ **LEFT:** Betty Grable.

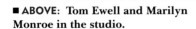

■ **ABOVE: Tom Ewell and Marilyn Monroe in the studio.**

■ **RIGHT: Robert Mitchum and Marilyn Monroe promoting the film *River Of No Return.***

home following a stint in prison to find his 10-year-old son Mark (Tommy Rettig), whom he left in the care of dance hall singer Kay (played by Monroe). The film received mixed reviews and Monroe later declared it was her worst film. Meanwhile, Mitchum is probably best remembered for his starring roles in film noir. He is also considered to be one of the early anti-heroes in film during the 1950s and 1960s.

Later in 1954, Monroe starred opposite Tom Ewell in *The Seven Year Itch*. It was a film that she wanted to make for 20th Century Fox. Ewell had begun his acting career in 1928 before enrolling at the Actors Studio

with Montgomery Clift. He was particularly renowned for his comic supporting roles until he began receiving more frequent calls to Hollywood. He starred in the Broadway production of *The Seven Year Itch* alongside Vanessa Brown and gave over 900 performances over three years. The stage role saw Ewell win a Tony Award in 1953 while he was presented with a Golden Globe for his film portrayal of Richard Sherman.

Bus Stop in 1956 was followed by *The Prince and the Showgirl*, where Monroe starred opposite British acting legend **Laurence Olivier**. The filming of the movie was far from easy for director and co-star Olivier, but he persevered with the American actress – and

■ **BELOW: Marilyn Monroe rolls up some pasta in a restaurant in San Francisco, during a dinner with actor Montgomery Clift.**

■ **ABOVE:** Marilyn Monroe with Sir Laurence Olivier at the Savoy Hotel, London.

■ **RIGHT:** Under the 1920s costumes and make-up of this pair of animated females, are two of Hollywood's best known she men, Jack Lemmon, (left) and Tony Curtis. They masquerade as women in an all-girl orchestra to escape gangsters hunting them in Billy Wilder's 1959 film, *Some Like It Hot*, in which they co-star with Marilyn Monroe.

the incessant interruptions of her drama coach – and finished with a film in which he describes Monroe as "quite wonderful". Olivier, as one of the most famous and revered actors of the 20ᵗʰ Century, played a wide variety of roles on stage and screen encompassing Greek tragedy to modern drama and everything in between. Olivier is regarded by many as the greatest actor of the 20ᵗʰ Century and his awards and honours are numerous including two Oscars, two honorary awards, five Emmy awards, three Golden Globes and BAFTA awards.

Following a break from Hollywood, Monroe returned to make the 1958 film *Some Like It Hot*, starring Jack Lemmon and Tony Curtis. Despite the break, Monroe was still suffering stage

■ **LEFT: Director Billy Wilder whispers words of advice to Marilyn Monroe.**
■ **RIGHT: Yves Montand and Marilyn Monroe in the studio promoting new film *Let's Make Love*.**

fright during the making of the film and her repeated lateness to the set was a complete nightmare for director Billy Wilder. Her behaviour was fairly hostile and included outbursts of profanity as well as a refusal to take part in filming. On some occasions, she insisted on retakes of scenes until she was satisfied – often refusing to take direction from Wilder. Monroe and Lemmon had quite a rapport, however, she is reported to have disliked Curtis after he made a joke about their love scenes. Although the making of the film had proved difficult (and Monroe suffered another miscarriage), the movie was a resounding success and certainly one of the best for Wilder. It was nominated for six Academy Awards and Monroe won a Golden Globe for Best Actress.

Although there was also work with the likes of Yves Montand, Montgomery Clift, Eli Wallach, Thelma Ritter and Dean Martin to name a few, one of the final performances that Monroe was to give came opposite co-star Clark Gable. *The Misfits* was to be the final film for both Hollywood icons. Arthur Miller began work on the script in 1956 and had developed the screenplay by 1960. Filming in Nevada began in July that same year where Monroe proved to be frequently ill. Her consumption of sleeping pills began to increase away from her doctor, Ralph Greenson, and she was eventually hospitalised for 10 days. Reports in newspapers told of a 'very ill Monroe'. Montgomery Clift had also suffered illness during filming while Thelma

■ **ABOVE:** Joey Bishop (left) and Frank Sinatra confer on stage before Sinatra's opening peformance at the Sands Hotel in Las Vegas, 10 June 1961. Seated ringside, left to right, are Marilyn Monroe, Elizabeth Taylor, Dean Martin and Mrs Martin.

■ **RIGHT:** Cast and principals of *The Misfits*, 1961. Front row, left to right: Montgomery Clift, Marilyn Monroe, Clark Gable. Back row, left to right: Eli Wallach, playwright Arthur Miller and director John Huston.

Ritter ended up in hospital with exhaustion. Gable was also reported as feeling unwell while on set. Just 10 days later, Gable was dead and his widow, Kay Gable, felt that the film had contributed to his death. Monroe did not publicly announce that she felt in some way responsible – Gable had spent hours waiting around for the actress to appear on set – but privately she expressed her regret at the poor treatment he had received. It seems that Kay Gable did not blame Monroe for the death of her husband; she invited the actress to the christening of Gable's son.

Chapter 5:
Filmography, Awards, Nominations and Honours

■ RIGHT: Marilyn Monroe poses in a scene from the movie *Something's Got To Give*. The movie was never completed and Monroe was fired from the set in July 1962.

Filmography

1947: *The Shocking Miss Pilgrim* – **Telephone operator**

1947: *Dangerous Years* – **Evie**

1948: *You Were Meant For Me* – **Monroe's part is unconfirmed (uncredited)**

1948: *Green Grass Of Wyoming* – **Extra (uncredited)**

1948: *Scudda Hoo! Scudda Hay!* – **Girl (uncredited)**

1948: *Ladies Of The Chorus* – **Peggy Martin**

1950: *A Ticket To Tomahawk* – **Clara (uncredited)**

1950: *The Asphalt Jungle* – **Angela Phinlay**

1950: *Right Cross* – **Dusky Ledoux (uncredited)**

1950: *The Fireball* – **Polly**

1950: *All About Eve* – **Miss Casswell**

1951: *Home Town Story* – **Iris Martin**

1951: *As Young As You Feel* – **Harriet**

1951: *Love Nest* – **Roberta Stevens**

1951: *Let's Make It Legal* – **Joyce Mannering**

1952: *Clash By Night* – **Peggy**

1952: *We're Not Married* – **Annabel Jones Norris**

1952: *Don't Bother To Knock* – **Nell Forbes**

1952: *Full House* – **Streetwalker**

1952: *Monkey Business* – **Lois Laurel**

1953: *Niagara* – **Rose Loomis**

1953: *Gentlemen Prefer Blondes* – **Lorelei Lee**

1953: *How To Marry A Millionaire* – **Pola Debevoise**

1954: *River Of No Return* – **Kay Weston**

1954: *There's No Business Like Show Business* – **Vicky**

1955: *The Seven Year Itch* – **The Girl**

1956: *Bus Stop* – **Cherie**

1957: *The Prince And The Showgirl* – **Elsie**

1959: *Some Like It Hot* – **Sugar Kane**

1960: *Let's Make Love* – **Amanda Dell**

1961: *The Misfits* – **Roslyn Taber**

1962: *Something's Got To Give* – **Ellen Wagstaff Arden**

■ **LEFT:** Marilyn Monroe at the Golden Globes.

■ **RIGHT:** Orchestra leader Ray Anthony recorded the song *Marilyn* and then gave a party in honour of the song's namesake, Marilyn Monroe. As part of the festivities Marilyn and Ray are seen here trying out a possible helicopter ride, but they never got off the ground.

■ **BELOW LEFT:** Marilyn Monroe and Rock Hudson with her award for Best Actress in a Comedy or Musical.

■ **BELOW RIGHT:** Queen Elizabeth II shakes hands with Marilyn.

■ **BOTTOM:** A 26ft-tall sculpture of Marilyn's most famous pose, located in downtown Chicago.

Awards, nominations and honours

1951   Henrietta Award: The Best Young Box Office Personality

1952   *Photoplay* Award: Fastest Rising Star of 1952

1952   *Photoplay* Award: Special Award

1952   *Look* (American Magazine) Achievement Award: Most Promising Female Newcomer of 1952

1953   Golden Globe Henrietta Award: World Film Favourite Female

1953   Sweetheart Of The Month (*Playboy*)

1953   *Photoplay* Award: Most Popular Female Star

1954   *Photoplay* Award for Best Actress: for *Gentlemen Prefer Blondes* and *How To Marry A Millionaire*

1956   BAFTA Film Award nomination: Best Foreign Actress for *The Seven Year Itch*

1956   Golden Globe nomination: Best Motion Picture Actress in Comedy or Musical for *Bus Stop*

1958   BAFTA Film Award nomination: Best Foreign Actress for *The Prince And The Showgirl*

1958   David di Donatello Award (Italian): Best Foreign Actress for *The Prince And The Showgirl*

1959   Crystal Star Award (French): Best Foreign Actress for *The Prince And The Showgirl*

1960   Golden Globe, Best Motion Picture Actress in Comedy or Musical for *Some Like It Hot*

1960   Honoured with a star on the Hollywood Walk of Fame, 6774 Hollywood Boulevard

1962   Golden Globe, World Film Favourite: Female

1999   Ranked as the sixth greatest female star of all time by the American Film Institute in their list 'AFI's 100 Years...100 Stars'

Chapter 6:
The Death of a Superstar

It seems that in the final year of her life, Monroe was suffering in terms of her private and professional life just as much as ever. She was flitting back and forth between New York and California and keeping her friends on the East and West coasts separate and generally unknown to each other, while she managed an effective role as a chameleon. It became apparent, however, that Monroe could well have been making plans to make her life permanently in California. It was also at this time that the worry of aging was beginning to rear its head. Despite the fact that Monroe liked the idea of old age and the sense of completeness that she felt older people gained through coming to terms with life experiences, the Hollywood icon was beginning to take notice of her own advancing years. It was worrying Monroe that she needed to start looking for more mature roles in Hollywood which would reflect her own changing appearance and talent.

Monroe was constantly threatening her psychiatrist with falling back into drugs and her sessions with Dr Ralph Greenson became ever more demanding and wearing. It was around this time, in June 1962, that she was fired from the set of *Something's Got To Give*, having only reported for work on 12 occasions out of a total of 35 days of production.

She found herself working once again at the Actors Studio in a one act play but, despite rave reviews and high hopes for her stage career, Monroe fell into an unsettling mood and once again found herself back in the office of Dr Greenson.

Greenson's advice was for Monroe to forget the Actors Studio and concentrate on 'fun' movies, and negotiations began with Fox over the summer of 1962 for her to finish filming *Something's Got To Give*. Between late June and early August, Monroe felt under incredible stress and was seeing Greenson almost every day. He, meanwhile, felt that he was defeated in his quest to help Monroe. At the same time, Monroe was posing for photographs with Bert Stern, in which she came across as both a strong and vulnerable personality depending on the angle of the picture. The pictures were taken over a number of sittings and at her last interview with Richard Merryman, she impressed with her professionalism. The photographs and interviews were meant to reprise her movie career. Having prepared carefully for the interview, Monroe saw the final words in print, two days before her death. It was the closest that the actress ever came to a final testament.

Contradictory evidence about the state of Monroe's physical and mental health surrounds her last few months and particularly her last few days.

Conspiracy theories

At the age of 36, Monroe was found dead on 5 August 1962 at her Brentwood home in Los Angeles, California. It was 4.25am when her psychiatrist, Dr Greenson, placed a call to LAPD

police sergeant Jack Clemmons to say that the star was dead. An autopsy by Dr Thomas Noguchi found Chloral hydrate and Nembutal in Monroe's system and as coroner he recorded 'acute barbiturate poisoning' as the cause of death. It was cited as possible suicide.

However, the conspiracy theories started almost the moment Monroe's death was publicly announced. Many were as a result of the strange circumstances surrounding her death and the timeline that elapsed after her body was found. John and Robert Kennedy were suggested as

■ **RIGHT: Dr Ralph Greenson.**

possible perpetrators, especially as it was reported that the last person that Monroe called was the president, but others were also implicated in the conspiracy

theories including the Mafia and the CIA. Her final hours – especially between 7.30pm on 4 August and 3.30am the following day when her body was found – have been surrounded by endless speculation. However, a further examination of the original autopsy report, around 20 years after her death, failed to highlight anything different from the initial findings and the Los Angeles District Attorney's office concluded that Dr Noguchi's autopsy of 'possible suicide' as a result of a drug overdose was sound.

The aftermath

After her death, Monroe was interred at the Westwood Village

■ ABOVE: Director George Cukor shares a laugh with Marilyn Monroe on the set of *Something's Got To Give*.

■ LEFT: A police officer points to an assortment of medicine bottles on the table beside the bed (right) of Marilyn Monroe's home in Los Angeles 5 August 1962, where she was found dead. Monroe was 36 years old.

■ RIGHT: Joe DiMaggio, second husband of Marilyn Monroe, enters the offices of the Westwood Village Mortuary in Los Angeles to assist in making final arrangements for Miss Monroe's funeral.

MARILYN MONROE

Memorial Park cemetery, Los Angeles. Joe DiMaggio took control of funeral arrangements and only 31 close family and friends were invited to attend. Lee Strasberg delivered the eulogy over a casket of solid bronze (lined with champagne-coloured silk), while Whitey Snyder did Monroe's make-up. Wearing her favourite Pucci dress, Monroe was buried discreetly and quietly. For the 20 years following her death, DiMaggio sent red roses to be placed in the vase attached to the crypt encasing Monroe's coffin three times a week.

■ **ABOVE:** Joe DiMaggio (right) is comforted at the crypt by Mr and Mrs Sam Kindelcamp, former foster parents of Marilyn Monroe.

■ **BELOW:** Marilyn's crypt.

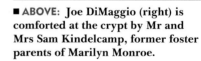

Chapter 7:
Quotes and Trivia

Quotes from Marilyn Monroe

We are all of us stars, and we deserve to twinkle.

If I'd observed all the rules I'd never have got anywhere.

It's not true that I had nothing on. I had the radio on.

I don't know who invented high heels, but all women owe him a lot.

I knew I belonged to the public and to the world, not because I was talented or even beautiful, but because I never had belonged to anything or anyone else.

I don't mind living in a man's world as long as I can be a woman in it.

To a reporter: Please don't make me a joke.

I've been on a calendar, but never on time.

Sex is a part of nature, I go along with nature.

I am invariably late for appointments... sometimes, as much as two hours. I've tried to change my ways but the things that make me late are too strong, and too pleasing.

Women who seek to be equal with men lack ambition.

The real lover is the man who can thrill you by kissing your forehead or smiling into your eyes or just staring into space.

Creativity has got to start with humanity and when you're a human being, you feel, you suffer.

I've never fooled anyone. I've let people fool themselves. They didn't

bother to find out who and what I was. Instead they would invent a character for me. I wouldn't argue with them. They were obviously loving somebody I wasn't.

Who said nights were for sleep?

If I'm a star, then the people made me a star.

It's nice to be included in people's fantasies but you also like to be accepted for your own sake.

I think that when you are famous every weakness is exaggerated.

A career is wonderful, but you can't curl up with it on a cold night.

I don't mind making jokes, but I don't want to look like one.

Trivia and facts about Marilyn

» Marilyn Monroe had pierced ears at a time when it was fashionable to wear clip-ons. Her ears were pierced at the age of 15.

» Jessica Rabbit, from the film *Who Framed Roger Rabbit* was modelled on Marilyn's size 14 figure.

» For Marilyn, the best side of her face was the right side.

» An FBI report allegedly claims that Marilyn Monroe was tricked into suicide.

» Her first paid modelling job was for $5.

» Marilyn washed her face up to 15 times a day to stop blemishes from appearing.

» Marilyn appeared on the cover of *Family Circle* in April 1946; it was her first appearance on the cover of a national magazine.

» The Monroe piercing, between the top lip and the nose is meant to look like a beauty spot and is inspired by the actress.

» Marilyn is believed to have had a one-night stand with Elvis Presley.

» Her favourite perfume was Chanel No 5.

» Marilyn was a fan of Louis Armstrong, Beethoven and Mozart.